DINOSAUR FOSSILS

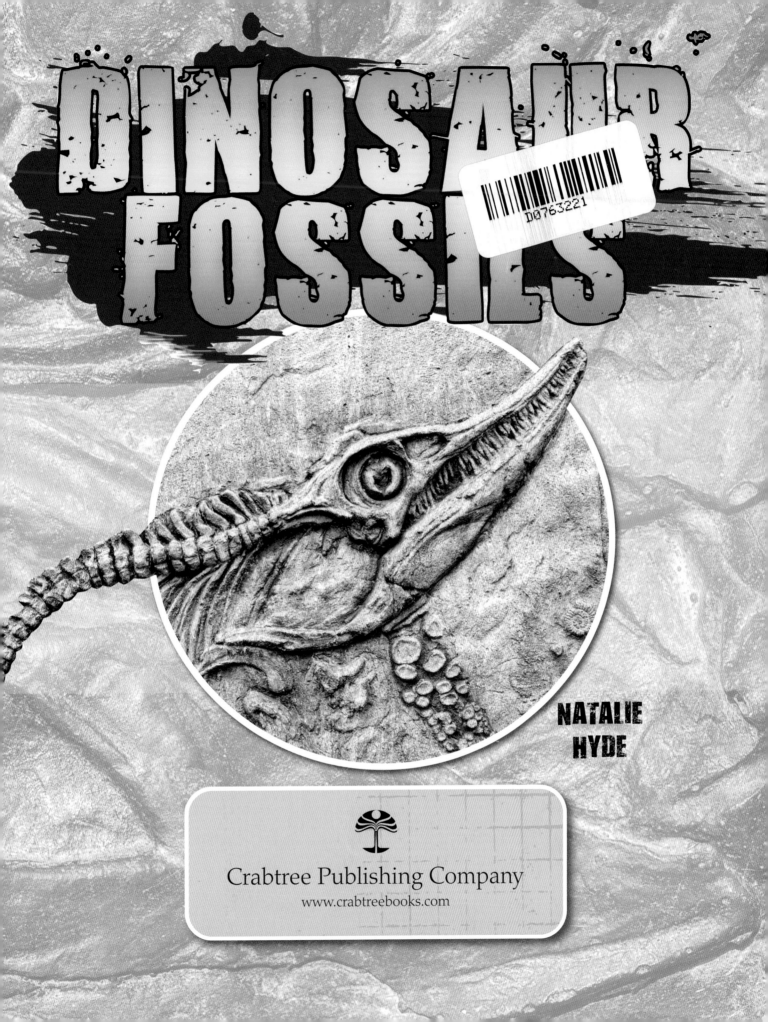

NATALIE HYDE

Crabtree Publishing Company

www.crabtreebooks.com

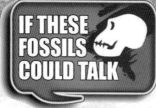

Author
Natalie Hyde

Publishing plan research and development
Reagan Miller

Editors
Adrianna Morganelli, Crystal Sikkens

Proofreader
Molly Aloian

Indexer
Wendy Scavuzzo

Design
Margaret Amy Salter

Photo research
Margaret Amy Salter, Crystal Sikkens

**Production coordinator
and prepress technician**
Samara Parent

Print coordinator
Margaret Amy Salter

Photographs
Associated Press: Will Kincaid: page 11
Science Source: Francois Gohier: page 8 (bottom); Francois
  Gohier / Photo Researchers, Inc.: page 15 (left); Laurie
  O'Keefe: page 22; Sinclair Stammers: page 27 (top)
Thinkstock: title page; pages 4-5 (bottom), 16 (right)
Wikimedia Commons: public domain: page 5 (top); © United
  States Geological Survey: page 9 (top); © Daderot: page 9
  (bottom); © Nobu Tamura: page 13 (bottom); © Mathew
  Brady: page 15 (right); © Sebastian Wallroth: page 17
  (bottom); © Mark Witton and Darren Naish: page 20;
  © Bruce McAdam: page 23 (right)
© Natursports/Shutterstock: page 7
All other images by Shutterstock

Library and Archives Canada Cataloguing in Publication

Hyde, Natalie, 1963-, author
    Dinosaur fossils / Natalie Hyde.

(If these fossils could talk)
Includes index.
Issued in print and electronic formats.
ISBN 978-0-7787-1262-6 (bound).--ISBN 978-0-7787-1266-4
(pbk.).--ISBN 978-1-4271-8956-1 (pdf).--ISBN 978-1-4271-8952-3
(html)

    1. Dinosaurs--Juvenile literature. I. Title.

QE861.5.H93 2013   j567.9   C2013-905233-X
                                          C2013-905234-8

Library of Congress Cataloging-in-Publication Data

Hyde, Natalie, 1963-
  Dinosaur fossils / Natalie Hyde.
    pages cm. -- (If these fossils could talk)
  Includes index.
  ISBN 978-0-7787-1262-6 (reinforced library binding : alk. paper) -- ISBN
  978-0-7787-1266-4 (pbk. : alk. paper) -- ISBN 978-1-4271-8956-1 (electronic
  pdf : alk. paper) -- ISBN 978-1-4271-8952-3 (electronic html : alk. paper)
  1. Dinosaurs--Juvenile literature. 2. Fossils--Juvenile literature. I. Title.

  QE861.5.H94 2014
  567.9--dc23
                                          2013033211

Crabtree Publishing Company

www.crabtreebooks.com   1-800-387-7650   Printed in Canada/092013/BF20130815

**Published in Canada
Crabtree Publishing**
616 Welland Ave.
St. Catharines, Ontario
L2M 5V6

**Published in the United States
Crabtree Publishing**
PMB 59051
350 Fifth Avenue, 59th Floor
New York, New York 10118

**Published in the United Kingdom
Crabtree Publishing**
Maritime House
Basin Road North, Hove
BN41 1WR

**Published in Australia
Crabtree Publishing**
3 Charles Street
Coburg North
VIC 3058

CONTENTS

A Giant Discovery 4

Fossil Formation 6

Trace Fossils 8

Dinosaur Mummies 10

Tiny Relics 12

Massive Monsters 14

Deadly Dinosaurs 16

Polar Dinosaurs 18

Flying Reptiles 20

Behave Yourself! 22

The Great Dying 24

Newest Discoveries 26

Get Cracking! 28

Glossary 30

Learning More 31

Index 32

A GIANT DISCOVERY

Dinosaurs haven't lived on Earth for millions of years. How can we possibly learn about creatures that don't exist anymore? How did they live? What did they eat? What did they look like?

PRESERVED REMAINS

All these answers can be found in dinosaur fossils. Fossils are **preserved** remains of any living organism. They can be **mineralized** parts of a body or an imprint of its shape. A fossil can even be a whole body trapped in a substance that prevents it from rotting.

FOSSIL EXPERTS

Paleontologists are scientists that find and study fossils. The different types of fossils and the locations where they are found are clues that help them unlock the mysteries of long-gone creatures. Some dinosaurs were as small as a pigeon. Others were as large as a blue whale.

Some dinosaurs walked on two legs and some walked on four. Some were quick and others lumbered along slowly.

William Buckland was the English paleontologist who first used the term "Dinosauria," Greek for "terrible lizard," in 1842. He created life-size models of what he thought dinosaurs looked like. He even hosted a New Years Eve dinner inside a concrete lizard-like *Iguanodon*.

WHAT HAPPENED?

The fossil record shows us that dinosaurs ruled Earth for about 165 million years. About 65 million years ago, they became extinct. Paleontologists look at these fossils to discover why this happened.

FACT FILE The first dinosaur bones that were found were **misidentified** because no one knew yet that dinosaurs had existed. In England, in 1676, a large thigh bone (femur) was discovered. People believed it was from a giant human being.

FOSSIL FORMATION

Fossils are only found in sedimentary rock. This type of rock forms when layers of silt, sand, and mud build up at the bottom of lakes, rivers, or oceans. Over time, the weight of the layers turns the sediment into rock. Any organic material caught in the layers becomes fossilized.

WHAT'S LEFT?

Most dinosaur fossils are bones and teeth because these are two of the hardest substances in a dinosaur's body. When a dinosaur dies and is buried, rock-like minerals can slowly enter the dinosaur's body and turn the bone or **enamel** into rock.

Fossils are also created when the shape of the dinosaur is pressed into soft clay or mud. Once the dinosaur's body **decomposes**, a detailed impression is left behind. This fossil is called a mold.

The bones in a dinosaur's body make up its skeleton. Most dinosaur skeletons have several hundred different bones.

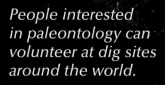

People interested in paleontology can volunteer at dig sites around the world.

DINO MUMMIES

Sometimes dinosaur bodies dry out completely and the skin shrinks around the bones, creating a mummy. Mummified dinosaurs are very important because they give us an idea of what the skin of dinosaurs looked like.

FACT FILE The oldest dinosaur fossils are of a small meat-eater found in South America that lived 230 million years ago. Recently, new fossils have been found in Tanzania, Africa, that may be even older.

THE DATING GAME

Paleontologists date fossils by looking at the rock in which they are found and how deep they are buried. Elements in rock, such as Uranium-235, break down over time, and scientists can use this to measure how old the rock is that lies under and above the fossil. They are careful to remember that sometimes fossils can be moved by mountain-building or glaciers long after dinosaurs became extinct.

How do paleontologists date dinosaur fossils?

TRACE FOSSILS

As dinosaurs moved, ate, and slept, they left behind traces of these activities. Dinosaur trace fossils, including footprints, nests, and claw marks, give paleontologists a glimpse into the lives and habits of dinosaurs.

WALK THIS WAY

Dinosaur tracks or footprints have been found on every continent except Antarctica. Two or more footprints are called a trackway or trail. Trackways can show whether a dinosaur was walking, running, or wading, and whether it walked on two or four legs. The depth of the prints can give clues to the weight of the dinosaur.

A group of trackways heading in the same direction could point to a **migration** route. Many clusters of tracks around a tree impression could suggest a feeding group. Trackways of different species moving at a run could be an ancient chase scene.

This group of Ornithopod dinosaur tracks were found in Denver, Colorado.

DINO DUNG

Coprolites are fossilized poop. These fossils help paleontologists understand the diet of dinosaurs. A coprolite full of plant material would point to a **herbivore**. Animal skin and bones in a coprolite would suggest a **carnivore**. The types of plant material can also help paleontologists learn what the environment looked like at the time the dinosaur ate its meal.

EGGS-ACTLY

Fossilized eggs have shown scientists that dinosaurs laid up to 20 eggs at a time. **Embryos** have been found inside some dinosaur eggs. Scientists were surprised at how fast they grew.

FACT FILE

The most famous coprolite was found in Saskatchewan, Canada. It is 17 inches (43 centimeters) long, and six inches (15 cm) wide. It contains bones and blood, which has led researchers to believe that it may be from a *Tyrannosaurus rex*.

This large nest of fossilized dinosaur eggs is on display at the Kunming Natural History Museum of Zoology in China.

DINOSAUR MUMMIES

Dinosaur mummies are extremely rare. A mummy is a body whose skin, and sometimes organs, have been preserved. Only four mummified dinosaurs have ever been found. Dinosaur mummification is unusual because many conditions have to be just right for the soft parts of a body to be preserved.

MUMMY IN THE MAKING

To form a mummy, the dinosaur's dead body had to be quickly covered or preserved before it began to decompose. This can happen in very hot, dry air, which dries out the body, similar to the royal mummies found in Egypt. It can also occur if the body is covered soon after death with wet soil that keeps out tissue-eating **bacteria**.

While Egyptian mummies have lasted thousands of years, dinosaur mummies have lasted millions!

DAKOTA

Paleontologists believe that this type of quick burial helped preserve a hadrosaur found in North Dakota. Named Dakota, it still had skin covering parts of its tail, arms, and legs. The amount of muscles in its hind end proved they it was much faster than scientists thought. It may even have been faster than a *T. rex*!

Amateur teenage paleontologist Tyler Lyson found the dinosaur mummy, Dakota, on his uncle's farm in 1999, when he was just 16 years old. He saw that the fossil included skin and knew then that he had found something special.

Visitors at the North Dakota Heritage Center have an opportunity to view the tail of Dakota.

LEONARDO

An even more amazing mummy dinosaur was discovered after Dakota. Named Leonardo, this mummified *Brachylophosaurus* was an almost complete dinosaur. Leonardo not only had its skin, scales, and footpads, but it had mummified and fossilized internal organs, too. Paleontologists found its last meal still in its stomach and could identify the plants that existed when Leonardo was alive.

11

TINY RELICS

When we think of dinosaur fossils, we often picture the massive bones of a towering sauropod. But were all dinosaurs giants? Not at all. In fact, some dinosaurs were no larger than a chicken.

LOOKING GOOD

Small fossils are not as common as larger ones. The dead body of such a small dinosaur is more likely to be eaten by a **scavenger**, and small, light bones are more likely to be crushed before they can fossilize. A few small dinosaur fossils have survived, however, and paleontologists learn a lot by studying them.

MICRORAPTORS

Microraptors were small four-winged, flying dinosaurs. Their name comes from a combination of the words "micro"—meaning small—and "raptor"—meaning one who seizes. They snacked on small mammals, birds, and fish. They had black feathers that appeared blue similar to crows. Some paleontologists believe the long feathers on their arms and legs allowed them to glide easily.

ANCIENT ROADRUNNER?

Another small dinosaur was the *Microceratus*, meaning "small-horned." This plant-eater was two feet (24 inches) long with a sharp beak and a little **frill**, or bony plate, on the back of its head. It was a speedy runner on its two long legs. This probably helped it avoid getting stepped on by larger, clumsier dinosaurs.

FRILLS

Paleontologists have used the fossils from small dinosaurs to learn the true use of special features such as bony frills on skulls. In some species, scientists were able to see that these features were used for display and not for protection.

*Paleontologists believe not all small skeletons were small dinosaurs. They now believe many of these smaller species are actually **juveniles** of larger species.*

FACT FILE

The ancestor of one of the biggest mammals alive today—whales, was a small land-dwelling four-footed animal that looked a lot like a modern dog. Scientists know the *Pakicetus* is related to whales because of the unique structure of its inner ears.

MASSIVE MONSTERS

The fossil record shows us that millions of years ago, huge dinosaurs roamed Earth. Some, like the Sauroposeidon, **were 60 feet (18 meters) tall and weighed as much as 15 elephants!**

LARGE HERBIVORES

The largest dinosaurs were sauropods. Fossils of sauropods have been found on every continent, including Antarctica. These slow-moving plant-eaters had very tiny brains. They had long necks to reach leaves at the tops of trees and long tails for balance.

BIG AND BIGGER!

One single vertebra (bone from the spine) from an *Argentinosaurus* is 5 feet (1.5 m) long. The largest skull ever found belonged to a *Torosaurus* and was 8 feet (2.4 m) long. But even these massive reptiles were still not as big as the blue whale living today!

Some sauropods had spines along their backs, such as the Brachiosaurus, and others had clubs on their tails.

BIG BONES

Working with such massive fossils can be difficult. Rock hammers or sometimes even **jackhammers** are needed to cut the stone around the bone. Plaster-coated burlap strips cover the top and bottom of the fossil once it is free to protect it during transport. Helicopters are used to move some of the bigger fossils.

A careless paleontologist named Othniel Marsh was in a hurry to beat other scientists to find the most dinosaurs. When he found a huge skeleton with no head, he attached it to the skull of another dinosaur and named it *Apatosaurus*. He later found another skeleton that looked like a different creature, so he named it *Brontosaurus*. It was actually just another *Apatosaurus*, but with the correct skull! The *Brontosaurus* was the only dinosaur that did not die out—because it never actually existed.

The pelvis of a Tyrannosaurus rex wrapped in plaster-coated burlap is being lowered down a hill.

Why was a sauropod's long neck and tail useful?

DEADLY DINOSAURS

One thing that the fossil record makes very clear is that many of these dinosaurs were fierce predators. There is evidence that they were built to hunt, grab, and kill prey.

ALL THE BETTER TO EAT YOU WITH!

Fossil teeth tell a story to paleontologists. Plant-eaters had spoon- or leaf-shaped teeth that were good for stripping leaves. Predators had sharp, pointed teeth that could tear flesh and crush bones. The *Tyrannosaurus rex* had 50 or 60 thick, sharp, cone-shaped teeth.

FIGHTING FOSSILS

The *Talos sampsoni* had a large claw on its foot. Scientists believe it might have been used to fight **rival** dinosaurs. It was sharp enough to puncture tough skin or maybe provide extra grip to climb up the back of a bigger dinosaur.

A T. rex tooth found in the tailbone of a hadrosaur proved that the "king of dinosaurs" was a fierce predator.

NIGHT STALKER

The deadliest dinosaur wasn't always the largest. The *Troodon* only weighed about 150 pounds (68 kilograms), but it had a much bigger brain, which meant it was a smarter hunter than most other dinosaurs. Its large eyes also helped it to see and hunt at night.

COLOSSAL CROC

Imagine a **prehistoric** crocodile that is as long and as heavy as a school bus, hiding in a river or stream ready to attack. That was the *Sarcosuchus*, also known as the "Super Croc."

The Super Croc had a large bulb on the tip of its nose. Scientists think it might have been to help it communicate or give it a better sense of smell.

FACT FILE

Stygimoloch, which means "demon from the river Styx" had the boniest head with several spikes and horns, some up to four inches (10 cm) long.

POLAR DINOSAURS

One hundred million years ago, Africa, India, Australia, and South America were connected to Antarctica. This landmass, called Gondwana, drifted south until it was inside the Antarctic Circle. The fact that similar fossils are found in these areas helps prove the theory of continental drift.

SEEING IN THE DARK

The tilt of Earth at the time meant that Gondwana has six weeks of total darkness each year. Dinosaur skull fossils found here show that small plant-eaters had huge eye sockets for larger eyes. Larger eyes helped them see during the long period of darkness.

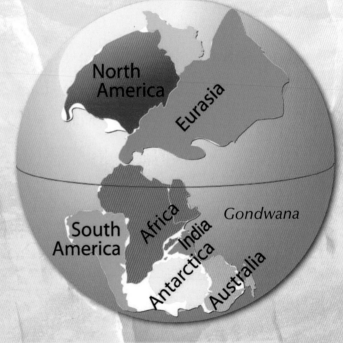

NOTEWORTHY NAMES

In 1980, Patricia Rich and her husband Thomas discovered an ancient river channel in Australia that was full of fossils of dinosaurs that once lived in polar regions. They named it Dinosaur Cove. Two of the new species of dinosaurs found there were named after their children, Leaellyn and Tim: *Leaellynasaura amicagraphica* and *Timimus hermani*.

A TOUGH JOB

Fossil-hunting in Antarctica is very difficult because there is **permafrost**. Permafrost is ground that is always frozen, even in the few summer months. This makes it difficult to free a fossil. Also, if the ground thaws slightly and freezes again it can crack bones into pieces, making them hard to recognize.

COLD-BLOODED?

Recently, bones of larger sauropods, like *Ankylosaurs*, have been discovered in Antarctica. Scientists question whether dinosaurs really were cold-blooded, as they had believed. Cold-blooded animals, such as snakes, use the Sun to heat their bodies. If dinosaurs were cold-blooded, how could they survive in the cold, polar darkness?

plesiosaur

FACT FILE

A skeleton of a *plesiosaur* was found in Antarctica. *Plesiosaurs* were **marine** reptiles that had long necks and paddle-like flippers. This fossil shows the climate of Antarctica might have been very different millions of years ago.

FLYING REPTILES

Pterosaurs took to the skies over 230 million years ago. These winged creatures lived among the dinosaurs and even went extinct around the same time, but they were not dinosaurs—they were flying reptiles.

TONS OF TEETH

Fossil footprints from *pterosaurs* show that they could walk on four feet, something like bats. Skull fossils show that *pterosaurs* had long, narrow heads. Some show about 90 long, slender cone-shaped teeth in their mouths.

LARGE WINGS

The *Pterodactylus* is a type of *pterosaur*. The name means "winged finger" in Greek. The wings were skin and muscle that stretched from an extra-long finger to their ankles. Some paleontologists think the wings might have been used for gliding more than flapping.

The Quetzalcoatlus is one of the largest flying creatures ever. Unlike other pterosaurs, it did not have teeth. Instead, it had a long, sharp beak with fur-like fuzz on its body.

SMALL AND LARGE

One of the smallest *pterosaur* fossils was found recently in China. The *Nemicolopterus crypticus* had a wingspan of only 10 inches (25 cm). The *Quetzalcoatlus northropi* had a wingspan of 35 feet (10 m)!

LEATHERY EGGS

Fossilized eggs of *pterosaurs* show that they were more like the eggs of modern reptiles and not like bird eggs. They were leathery and flexible, like the eggs of a turtle or crocodile, not hard and easily cracked like chicken eggs.

GONE!

It would seem natural that modern birds would have **evolved** from *pterosaurs*, but they didn't. *Pterosaurs* died out about 65 million years ago. Scientists believe modern birds evolved from land-based dinosaurs.

Pterodactyls are a type of *pterosaur*. Were *pterodactyls* the ancestors of modern pelicans? Why or why not?

pterodactyls

pelican

BEHAVE YOURSELF!

It is difficult for paleontologists to know exactly how dinosaurs lived, moved, fought, or protected their young. They can only look at the fossil record left behind for clues. New technologies are helping scientists better understand dinosaur behavior.

TRAVELING IN HERDS

Scientists have found the trackways of hundreds or even thousands of duck-billed dinosaurs together, which show that they moved in large herds, like the buffalo or bison. Sauropod footprints in England also show that several different species traveled together.

NEST NURSERY

Maiasaur nests found together in Montana give the idea that some dinosaurs created "nurseries" where the females could watch many nests at once. Skeletons found at the nests show that the youngsters didn't leave until they were at least 3 feet (1 m) long.

Adult Maiasaurs *cared for and fed their young until they were strong enough to find their own food.*

HANGING OUT

Paleontologists think that young dinosaurs may have formed social groups that "hung out" together. A fossil find in Mongolia showed the remains of over 20 *Sinornithomimus*, who were all between one and seven years old when they were trapped in mud together.

EAT UP!

The *Majungatholus* was known as the **cannibal** dinosaur. Paleontologists found the dinosaur's **distinct** tooth marks on other *Majungatholus* bones in Madagascar.

NAP TIME

The fossil of a two-legged, bird-like meat-eater, the *Mei*, was found with its head tucked under its arm. Paleontologists believe they may have slept this way to rest their neck muscles, like some modern birds do.

What evidence do scientists have that dinosaurs were caring parents?

The resting position of the Mei fossil indicates the dinosaur was buried instantly, possibly by volcanic ash.

sleeping duck

THE GREAT DYING

Paleontologists are looking to the fossil record to find out what happened to the dinosaurs. It is clear that they died out, but the question is why? Scientists have several theories.

IMPACT!

Scientists have found evidence that a meteor at least 6 miles (10 km) wide hit Earth near the Yucatan Peninsula in Mexico about 66 million years ago. An **impact** that large would cause a lot of damage. It could bring on **tsunamis** and earthquakes, killing the dinosaurs or their food supply.

ICE AGE

Another theory is that there were many volcanic eruptions around that time. The ash from the volcanoes would block the sunlight, killing plants, and changing the climate. This may have brought on an **ice age**. The land would then be covered in snow and the fresh water would be frozen. With a shortage of food and water, dinosaurs could become extinct over time.

DEADLY DISEASE

Some scientists believe disease wiped out the dinosaurs. A deadly **virus** may have spread quickly, causing them to die out.

The Great Dying is a mass extinction, which means more than 50 percent of all known living species become extinct in a short period of time.

STILL UNKNOWN

None of these theories have been proven. In fact, a combination of all of these theories may be the cause for the extinction. No one knows why dinosaurs became extinct, and other animals survived. Researchers are still looking for answers today.

NEWEST DISCOVERIES

There are still a lot of questions to be answered about dinosaurs. Paleontologists are finding new dinosaur fossils all the time and each one helps them to better understand how dinosaurs looked, behaved, and evolved.

DINO DOGGY PADDLE

Paleontologists have found evidence that dinosaurs paddled and swam long distances. A series of fossil footprints in an ancient river bottom in China show that it was once a major highway for dinosaurs. Among the footprints are claw marks left by the tips of two-legged dinosaurs, who were swimming along the river with their toes just touching the bottom.

3D DINOSAURS

Scientists are using 3D imaging to find out what dinosaurs really looked like. Just like **forensic** labs reconstruct faces from skulls, new technology is letting paleontologists do the same for dinosaur skulls.

Researchers hope to create realistic images to get a better idea of how dinosaurs looked and moved.

FEATHERED DINOSAURS

New fossils discovered in the Badlands of Alberta show the first feathered dinosaurs of North America. The fossils of three ostrich-like dinosaurs that lived 75 million years ago were covered in feathers. Paleontologists noticed that the feathers on the juvenile were different from the two adults. This shows the feathers grew and changed during the life of these non-flying dinosaurs.

(above) The first feathered dinosaur fossils were of dromeosaurs, or raptors, found in China. Researchers believe they could be the link between dinosaurs and birds.

(below) The Badlands of Alberta are one of the richest dinosaur fossil sites in the world.

GET CRACKING!

Make your own dinosaur egg fossils with babies inside!
You will need:

1/2 cup (118 ml) coffee grounds (used or instant)

1/2 cup (118 ml) sand

1/2 cup (118 ml) salt

small, plastic dinosaurs or other "artifacts"

1 cup (237 ml) water

1 cup (237 ml) flour

large bowl

baking sheet

Ask an adult to help you prepare the eggs.

1. Preheat the oven to 250 °F (120 °C).

2. Mix the dry ingredients together in a large bowl.

3. Add the water a little at a time until you get a dough-like consistency.

4. Take a handful of the dough and flatten it.

5. Place a dinosaur on the dough and fold the dough around the dinosaur, sealing it up.

6. Mold your dough into the shape of eggs.

7. Place the eggs on a baking sheet and bake for 15 minutes.

8. Leave overnight to finish drying. If they are still a bit soft, put them back in the oven again for a few minutes.

Become a paleontologist and **excavate** your fossil eggs to find the dinosaur inside!

GLOSSARY

bacteria One-celled organisms; some can cause disease

cannibal An animal that feeds on the flesh of its own species

carnivore An animal that eats meat

continental drift The slow movement of the continents

decomposes Decays; rots away

distinct Recognizably different

embryos Unborn or unhatched offspring

enamel The hard, white coating of teeth

evolved Developed gradually over time

forensic Using scientific methods to investigate crimes

herbivore An animal that eats plants

ice age A time during which Earth's temperature dropped to freezing

impact The collision of two objects

jackhammer An air-powered hammer or drill

juveniles Youngsters

marine Living in the sea or ocean

migration Moving from one place to another

mineralized When cells are replaced with minerals

misidentified Recognized incorrectly

organic Living matter

permafrost A layer of ground that stays frozen all year round

predators Animals that hunt and eat others for food

prehistoric A time before written records

preserved Kept in its original state

rival Someone who competes with another

sauropod A large, four-legged dinosaur with a long neck and tail

scavenger An animal that eats dead or dying animals or plants

spine A pointed, bony structure

tsunamis Enormous ocean waves caused by earthquakes or volcanoes

virus A small organism that can cause disease

LEARNING MORE

FURTHER READING:

Connors, Kathleen. *Dinosaur Fossils*. Gareth Stevens Publishing, 2012.

Eldredge, Niles.*The Fossil Factory: A Kid's Guide to Digging Up Dinosaurs, Exploring Evolution, and Finding Fossils.* HarperCollins Canada, 1998.

Long, John. *Dinosaurs*. Simon & Schuster, 2007.

MacLeod, Elizabeth. *Monster Fliers*. Kids Can Press, 2010.

Ray, Deborah. *Dinosaur Mountain*. FSG Kids, 2010.

WEBSITES:

Use a special machine to make your own dinosaur fossil!
www.wonderville.ca/asset/fossil-fabricator

Learn about dinosaur fossils, eggs, bones, and skeletons:
www.sciencekids.co.nz/sciencefacts/dinosaurs/fossilseggs.html

The Smithsonian National Museum of Natural History on dinosaurs:
http://paleobiology.si.edu/dinosaurs/info/everything/what.html

An online book about dinosaurs:
www.enchantedlearning.com/subjects/dinosaurs/

INDEX

3D imaging, 26
Ankylosaurs, 19
Antarctica, 19
Apatosaurus, 15

bacteria, 10
Badlands, 27
birds, 21
bony frills, 13
Buckland, William, 5

cannibal dinosaur, 23
carnivores, 9, 16–17
China, 21, 26, 27
claws, 16, 26
coprolites, 9
crocodile, 17

Dakota, 11
dating fossils, 7
Dinosaur Cove, 18
disease, 25

eggs, 9, 21
evolving, 21, 26
extinction theories, 24–25
eyes, 17, 18

feathers, 12, 27
flying dinosaurs, 20–21, 27

footprints, 8, 20, 22, 26
fossil formation, 6–7

Gondwana, 18

hadrosaur, 11
herbivores, 9, 13, 14

ice age, 24

large dinosaurs, 14–15
largest skull, 14
Leonardo, 11
Lyson, Tyler, 11

Maiasaurs, 22
make a dinosaur egg, 28–29
Marsh, Othniel, 15
Mei, 23
meteor, 24
Microceratus, 13
Microraptors, 12
misidentified bones, 5
mold fossils, 6
moving bones, 15
mummies, 7, 10–11

nests, 9, 22
night vision, 17, 18

oldest fossils, 7

Pakicetus, 13
paleontologists, 4, 5, 15
plesiosaurs, 19
poop, 9
predators, 16–17
pterosaurs, 20–21

Quetzalcoatlus, 20, 21

raptors, 12, 27
Rich, Patricia and Thomas, 18

size, 4, 12–13, 14–15
skin, 7, 9, 10, 11, 16, 20
skulls, 13, 14, 16, 17, 20
small dinosaurs, 12–13
social groups, 23
Stygimoloch, 17
Super Croc, 17
swimming, 26

teeth, 16, 20
trace fossils, 8–9
Troodon, 17
Tyrannosaurus rex, 9, 11, 15, 16

whales, 13, 14